KT-433-246

smoothies
and other blended
drinks

smoothies
and other blended
drinks

elsa petersen-schepelern
photography by
james merrell

RYLAND
PETERS
& SMALL
London New York

Art Director **Jacqui Small**

Art Editor **Penny Stock**

Editor **Elsa Petersen-Schepelern**

Photography **James Merrell**

Food Stylist **Bridget Sargeson**

Stylist **Ben Kendrick**

Production **Kate Mackillop**

My thanks to Norah Meany, Jenny Merrell, Peter Bray,
Clare Gordon-Smith, Tessa Kerwood, Grant Stanton,
Louise Sherwin-Stark and Jack Sargeson

**Note: Take care – not all blenders or food processors
are designed to crush ice. If yours isn't, crush the ice
separately and spoon into the serving glass before
adding the smoothie mixture.
Ice cream scoop measurements used in this book are
medium, unless otherwise specified.**

First Published in Great Britain in 1997
by Ryland Peters & Small
Kirkman House, 12-14 Whitfield Street, London W1T 2RP
www.rylandpeters.com

Text © Elsa Petersen-Schepelern 1997
Design and photographs © Ryland Peters & Small 1997
10 9 8 7 6 5
Printed and bound in China

ISBN 1 900518 20 1

A CIP record for this book is available from the British Library

smoothies
and other blended
drinks

Blenders, food processors and juicers have made life much easier and more exciting for us all. Many different kinds of drinks are quickly assembled using any of these wonder machines. A blender, especially one that is strong enough to crush ice, can be used to mix smoothies, thickshakes, lassi yoghurt drinks and cocktails.

The drinks in this book are quickly made in any of these machines, and are based on the ingredients shown here; ice cream, milk, yoghurt, ice, fruit, sugar – as well as wine, spirits and liqueurs.

If you're watching your weight, you can use low-fat milk and yoghurt, as well as fresh fruit juice. Many are so delicious you won't even want to add any sugar at all.

If you're a chilli fiend – there's good news! Serve some of the yoghurt-based drinks – since capsaicin, the chemical in chillies that makes them hot, is fat-soluble rather than water-soluble, they'll quell the fires a little, and so allow you to keep munching!

6

chocolate mocha thickshake

Coffee and chocolate produces the classic mocha mixture. Make this smoothie stronger or sweeter to taste – heaven for chocoholics!

100 ml espresso coffee, chilled

125 g plain dark cooking chocolate,

or 2 tablespoons chocolate syrup

3-4 scoops vanilla ice cream

100 ml chilled milk, or to taste

sugar, to taste

to serve

whipped cream

chocolate curls

Place the coffee and chocolate together in a blender and whizz. Add the ice cream and whizz again. Add just enough milk to produce the desired consistency, whizz, taste and add sugar as needed.

Serve topped with a swirl of whipped cream and a sprinkle of chocolate curls.

Serves 1-2

ice cream

smoothies

passionfruit
thickshake with galliano

Passionfruit with Galliano liqueur is a terrific combination. If the Galliano hasn't survived your trip to Italy, use Grand Marnier instead. If you like your thickshake even thicker, add extra ice cream: if you like it smoother, add extra milk, to taste.

3 passionfruit, chilled

1 tablespoon Galliano

3 scoops ice cream

100 ml milk, or to taste

sugar, to taste

Scoop the pulp and seeds of 2 passionfruit into the blender, add the Galliano, ice cream and milk, then blend.
Taste, then add sugar and a little extra milk if preferred. Spoon the remaining passionfruit over the top, then serve.
Serves 1-2

11

This is a Vienna-coffee-style smoothie – add extra milk if you prefer your coffee creamier, or extra ice cream if you like to stand your spoon up in your coffee!

100 ml espresso coffee, chilled

1 tablespoon Drambuie (optional)

2 scoops vanilla ice cream

100 ml milk, or to taste

sugar, to taste

Place the coffee in a food processor or blender, with the Drambuie, if using. Add the ice cream and half the milk, then blend. Add sugar to taste, and add extra milk if you like your smoothie smoother.

Serves 1–2

coffee ice cream smoothie

ginger shake

If you're a ginger fan, this recipe will be your idea of heaven. Another treat for ginger fiends is what is called a 'Ginger Spider' in my native Australia. Place a big scoop of ice cream in a soda glass and top with ginger ale. Why a spider? I don't know – but I do know I'm terrified of them!

6 pieces stem ginger, in syrup

100 ml milk, or to taste

3 scoops ice cream

extra sugar, to taste

to serve (optional)

small scoops of ice cream

extra ginger, chopped

Place the ginger pieces, ice cream, milk and 6 tablespoons of the syrup in a blender, then purée to a froth. Taste and add extra milk and sugar if preferred. Serve, decorated to taste with another small scoop of ice cream or some extra ginger, chopped.

Serves 1-2

strawberry liqueur smoothie

Old-time American soda jerks were experts at balancing a scoop of ice cream on the edge of the soda glass. If you're not, you could always try to balance yours on a teaspoon! Make endless variations of this recipe, matching the liqueur to the fruit – Eau de Fraises with strawberries, Framboise with raspberries, Poire William with pears, peach liqueur with peaches, and so on.

A variation on this recipe doesn't even need a blender – make a Strawberry Spider in a tall glass with a scoop of strawberry ice-cream, 1 tablespoon of liqueur or strawberry syrup, then top up with soda (preferably strawberry). Pour in the soda very carefully – it will fizz like mad!

250 g strawberries

1 tablespoon strawberry liqueur

3 scoops strawberry ice cream

100 ml milk, or to taste

1 small scoop strawberry ice cream, to serve

Place the first 4 ingredients in a blender and whizz. Add extra ice cream for a thicker smoothie, or extra milk, to taste. Serve with an extra small scoop of ice cream balanced on the edge of the glass (if possible).

Serves 1–2

a summer shake with the bright,
sweet scent of ripe berries

passionfruit meringue smoothie

A recipe based on the Pavlova – the national pudding of Australia and New Zealand. It was named in honour of the great Russian ballerina who toured Down Under in the 1920s, when travelling to such frontier territories required a good deal of fortitude. The Pavlova consists of a large meringue, topped with fresh fruit and whipped cream, then cut into slices like a cake. Passionfruit is almost always included as one of the fruits, plus strawberries in the cooler south of the country and fruits like papaya, mango and pineapple in the tropical north.

It can be changed according to which fruits are in season and is a particular treat for someone with a sweet tooth. Apply the same seasonal rules to this amazing drink and enjoy yourself!

Make the meringues yourself if you like—but it is much simpler to buy them.

2 small white meringues, about 5 cm in diameter

250 g strawberries (or other fruit in season)

2 passionfruit

3 scoops ice cream, or to taste

100 ml milk, or to taste

to serve (optional)

1 tablespoon whipped cream

pulp and seeds of 1 passionfruit

1 meringue, crumbled

Place the meringues, strawberries and milk in a blender or food processor, then whizz. Add the ice cream and the seeds and pulp of 2 passionfruit. Blend again. Taste and add extra milk if you like a thinner drink, or extra ice cream if you like it thicker.

Pour into tall glasses, and serve, topped with the crumbled meringue, passionfruit pulp and whipped cream, if using.

Serves 1–2

18

peach melba
shake

Another recipe with connections Down Under. Peach Melba is another of the world's great desserts, created by legendary French chef Escoffier in honour of the 19th Century Australian soprano, Dame Nellie Melba – who must have been something of a gourmet, since a number of famous dishes are named after her. This liquid variation is wonderful at any time of day.

2 poached peaches (canned or home-made)

50 g fresh raspberries

3 scoops vanilla ice cream

100 ml milk, or to taste

to serve (optional):

1 tablespoon crushed flaked almonds

1 tablespoon fresh raspberries

whipped cream

If poaching fresh peaches, place them in a saucepan, add 1 tablespoon of sugar per peach, and cover with water or white wine. Bring to the boil and simmer for about 6–10 minutes until tender. Cool, slip off the skins, then remove the stones and chill the fruit. Keep the syrup to sweeten the shake.

To make the shake, place the fruit, ice cream and milk in a blender or food processor and whizz until foaming. Add extra ice cream or mil, to taste. Serve, sprinkled with crushed almonds, raspberries or whipped cream.

Serves 1–2

Overleaf: Peach Melba shake (left) and Passionfruit Meringue smoothie (right).

A slimming but filling breakfast – full of flavour, packed with calcium and fibre, and very good for you! If you like your drinks less sweet, reduce the quantity of honey. You can also substitute other fruit in season, such as berries. Use chilled fruit to make smoothies – but never put bananas in the refrigerator – or anywhere near citrus fruit – they don't like it. They quickly turn black in the refrigerator, and become over-ripe in a flash if introduced to a citrus fruit.

banana and honey
breakfast smoothie

250 ml low-fat milk

250 ml low-fat yoghurt

2 tablespoons crushed ice

1 tablespoon honey

1 banana

1 tablespoon wheatgerm

Place all the ingredients in the blender and whizz. Add extra fruit if preferred.

Serves 2–4

yoghurt drinks

Lassis are a traditional yoghurt drink in India, served plain, sweet or salty – perfect coolers in hot weather. This is a very indulgent form of lassi – but you can take refuge in the fact that yoghurt and ginger are very calming for upset stomachs. Use low-fat yoghurt if you prefer, and substitute almost any fruit you have on hand, including non-tropical ones like pears, apricots or peaches. If you use ginger a lot, it's worth making a quantity of purée and keeping it in the refrigerator. Soak 250 g of fresh root ginger in water overnight, peel, then whizz in a food processor with a little water: it will keep for up to a month.

Place all the ingredients in a blender or food processor and purée. Serve, poured over crushed ice and garnished with mint.
Serves 2–3

flavoured yoghurt

250 ml peeled, deseeded papaya

250 ml crushed pineapple

or pineapple juice

1 banana

250–500 ml plain yoghurt

1 tablespoon puréed fresh ginger

juice and grated zest of 1 lime

to serve

crushed ice

sprigs of mint

tropical fruit lassi
with papaya ginger and lime

24

drinks are **India's** favourite coolers

vanilla or chocolate
yoghurt lassi

Yoghurt drinks are traditionally served with hot Indian curries, some of which can be amazingly spicy. Capsaicin, the chemical in chillies that makes them hot, is not water-soluble, so drinking water, alcohol or tea will not cool your mouth. Milk or yoghurt are the perfect antidote, so this is a wonderful drink to serve with any dish containing chillies.

In India, lassis are flavoured with rosewater, saffron, pistachio nuts or spices such as cardamom. Vanilla and chocolate flavours are more familiar to Western tastes, but you could also experiment and create your own.

300 ml plain low-fat yoghurt

300 ml skim milk

250 ml crushed ice (optional)

1 tablespoon sugar, or to taste

a choice of:

2 tablespoons chocolate syrup,

or a few drops of vanilla extract,

or 1 teaspoon each of rosewater and

crushed cardamom seeds

Place the yoghurt, milk and crushed ice in a blender or food processor and whizz. Add the chosen flavouring and whizz again. Taste and add sugar if preferred.

Serves 1–2

27

Mango, papaya or banana are perfect fruits to team with milk and yoghurt. More unusual is passionfruit and 1 teaspoon Grand Marnier or Galliano liqueur. Milk and yoghurt are great sources of calcium – use the low-fat kind if you're watching your waistline.

Yoghurt and bananas are very good if you have an upset stomach, so you might try this drink as a hangover cure!

The variation below, Savoury Yoghurt Lassi with Spices, is served as an accompaniment to spicy curry dishes all over India, instead of beer or wine. Salty drinks are very cooling in the searing heat of a true Indian summer!

Variation:

Savoury Yoghurt Lassi with Spices

Instead of the fruit and sugar listed in the main recipe, substitute 1 teaspoon crushed cumin seeds and salt to taste, then serve.

Serves 2–4

250 ml low-fat plain yoghurt

125 ml low-fat milk

6 large strawberries

choice of fruit, such as:

1 small punnet raspberries, or

250 g apricots or peaches, stoned

sugar, to taste

crushed ice, to serve

Place all the ingredients except the sugar and ice in the blender and process. Taste, add sugar if preferred, then pour into a glass filled with crushed ice.

Serves 2-4

fruit salad lassi with strawberries

29

coconut with cloves

To make your own coconut milk, place about 6 tablespoons desiccated coconut in a bowl and cover with milk or water. Let stand for 20 minutes, then press through a strainer. If you don't want to use coconut milk at all, substitute ordinary milk plus coconut syrup, or any kind of fruit syrup.

100 ml milk

250 ml coconut milk (see above)

3 scoops ice cream

1 teaspoon ground cloves

sugar, to taste

to serve (optional)

crushed ice

finely sliced fresh coconut

Place the milk, coconut milk, ice cream and cloves in the blender, and whizz until frothy. Taste and add sugar if required. Whizz again until the sugar has dissolved. Serve over crushed ice, topped with coconut.

Serves 1–2

asian flavours

pineapple apricot yoghurt smoothie

A recipe with ingredients from opposite ends of India – apricots from the romantic Vale of Kashmir in the shadow of the Himalaya and pineapples from the tropical south. Use fresh apricots if you like, but I find their sweetness is not to be relied upon.

6 fresh or dried apricots, stoned

250 ml fresh pineapple pieces or canned unsweetened pineapple

300 ml plain or Greek yoghurt

sugar, to taste

to serve

crushed ice

chopped fresh apricot (optional)

If using dried apricots, soak them overnight in cold water to cover.

Whizz the pineapple in a blender with the apricots and yoghurt. Sweeten to taste, then pour over crushed ice.

Serve, topped with chopped apricot, if using.

Serves 2–3

Coconut milk and bananas are a traditional Thai combination – I've added dark rum as an optional extra. The result is a Thailand-meets-the-Caribbean mixture! The mango variation (shown far right, recipe below) can be made with fresh mango, or canned Alphonso mango purée. Usually, I'm not an advocate of using other than fresh produce. However, if you can find canned Alphonso mango in an Asian market, buy it and try it. The Alphonso is famously the world's greatest mango – and believe me, it is! Indians are connoisseurs of mangoes – they have hundreds of varieties and use them fresh, cooked, juiced, turned into chutneys, cooked green with meat, served as salads and in countless other ways.

Variation:

Coconut Milk with Mango

Use 250 ml Alphonso mango purée or 1 large ripe fresh mango instead of the bananas and rum. Whizz until frothy and serve with a scoop of mango ice cream.

about 250 ml canned coconut milk

250 ml low-fat milk

2 ripe bananas

1 tablespoon dark rum

sugar, to taste

crushed ice, to serve

Place all the ingredients in the blender except the sugar and ice. Whizz, adding sugar and more rum, to taste. Pour over crushed ice and serve.

Serves 1–2

coconut banana shake

great **tropical** ingredients

give the taste of Thailand

pineapple and lime crush

Also delicious made with ice cream rather than yoghurt or coconut milk. If keeping cut pineapple in the refrigerator, first wrap it in clingfilm to prevent it tainting other foods. Fruit varies in sweetness, so taste the crush before serving and add sugar if necessary.

300 ml yoghurt or coconut milk

250 g chopped fresh ripe pineapple

juice and grated rind of 2 limes

250 ml crushed ice

sugar, to taste

to serve (optional):

finely sliced fresh coconut

1 scoop vanilla ice cream

Place the first 4 ingredients in a blender and whizz. Taste and add sugar if needed. Serve decorated with the fresh coconut or a scoop of ice cream, if preferred.

Serves 1–2

banana honey and soy milk smoothie

A good breakfast smoothie – and full of protein from the soy milk. It is quite sweet, so taste the mixture before adding any extra honey. Other fruits, such as strawberries, bananas or papaya, can be used instead of the banana.

1 banana

1 teaspoon honey

250 ml soy milk

250 ml crushed ice (optional)

sprigs of mint, to serve (optional)

Place the banana, honey and soy milk in a blender with the crushed ice, if using, and whizz. Serve, topped with sprigs of mint.

Serves 1

orange juice
and strawberry crush

A recipe that can be adapted for any fruit in season – just make sure to chill them all (except the banana). You can whizz them in a blender, or put them through a juice extractor if you prefer your drink a little smoother. If you use apples, remember to add the orange juice immediately, so they don't go brown.

1 banana

3 ripe apricots, stoned

6 ripe red strawberries

juice of 1 large orange

3 scoops ice cream

250 ml milk, or to taste

Place all the fruit in the blender with half the milk and whizz. Add the ice cream and remaining milk, to taste, and whizz again.

Serves 2

sodas and crushes

a perfect summer cooler

zippy with ginger

Indian and Moroccan sharbats are distantly related to the sherbets which are familiar to Westerners. They were introduced by the Moghul emperors who invaded India over its North West Frontier in the 16th century.

If you have a juice extractor, use it to make watermelon juice – though I must admit I prefer the thicker consistency produced by a food processor. You can buy ginger purée in supermarkets, but if you can't find it, just peel fresh ginger root and purée in a food processor with a little water or lemon juice, then freeze in small quantities for future use.

1 small, ripe watermelon, chilled

2 tablespoons ginger purée

(or more, to taste)

water (see method)

sugar, to taste

crushed ice, to serve

watermelon
and ginger
sharbat

Cut the watermelon in half, remove and discard the rind and seeds. Whizz the flesh in a food processor with the ginger. Add water if the mixture is too thick. Taste and add sugar if needed. Serve over crushed ice. Serves 2-4

Variation:

Almond Sharbat

Grind 125 g skinned almonds in a blender, adding a little water to make a smooth paste. Add a few drops of almond essence (optional), 500 ml water, crushed seeds from 8 green cardamom pods, 1 teaspoon rosewater (optional) and sugar to taste. Whizz, then taste and add more sugar if liked. Pour over crushed ice and serve.

41

Bananas and limes are typical South-east Asian ingredients, as is ginger, though not usually in this form. Lychees, if you can find them, make a delicious substitute for the bananas – they are sold either fresh or canned in Asian markets.

2–3 large bananas

grated zest and juice of 2 limes

ginger ale, to taste

crushed ice

sugar, to taste

Whizz the bananas in a blender with the lime zest and juice, and a little ginger ale. Taste and add sugar if liked. Place crushed ice in the bottom of each glass, pour over the mixture and top up with more ginger ale.
Serves 2

bananas and limes
with ginger ale

mint and ginger yoghurt soda

Mint and ginger make a gorgeous combination. Ginger purée is sold in some supermarkets – or make it yourself with fresh root ginger in a blender. Plain yoghurt has a wonderful lemony taste. I prefer this drink without sugar – so taste it first and decide for yourself.

300 ml plain or low-fat yoghurt
leaves from 4 sprigs fresh mint
2.5 cm piece of fresh ginger, grated,
or 1 tablespoon ginger purée
500 ml soda water, or to taste
sugar, to taste
crushed ice, to serve

Place the yoghurt, mint and ginger in a blender with about 100 ml soda water, and whizz. Add sugar if preferred. Place crushed ice in the bottom of each glass, pour over the mixture, then top up with soda water.
Serves 2–4

pineapple with Jamaican ginger beer

Ginger beer is a favourite drink in Jamaica. Put it together with fresh pineapple, and you have an utterly delicious thirst-quencher – the taste of the Caribbean through a straw! Try it mixed with other fresh fruit too, like very ripe peaches, papayas or apricots.

3 slices ripe fresh pineapple, chilled
about 300 ml ginger beer, chilled
about 250 ml crushed ice

Whizz the pineapple in a blender with the crushed ice and 2–3 tablespoons of ginger beer. Pour into tall glasses and top up with the remaining ginger beer.
Serves 1–2

spicy, sweet and cool – **ginger**, mint, pineapple and yoghurt

Freshly crushed tomato juice is a far cry from the commercial variety. There are many juicers and crushers available now, but if you don't have one, just whizz ripe tomatoes in your food processor or blender, then press through a strainer (hard work, but worth it!) Taste the juice before adding any sugar. Try this recipe if you grow your own fruit, or in the height of summer, when tomatoes are cheap, ripe and plentiful.

This method can also be used to produce fresh tomato soup (hot or cold), perhaps with a splash of chicken stock, and sprinkled with torn basil leaves. If serving hot, heat the soup just a little, to keep the fresh tomato flavor. To make tomato paste, reduce the pulp over a gentle heat.

1 kg tomatoes

lemon juice, to taste

salt and pepper, to taste

sugar (optional)

Tabasco sauce (optional)

crushed ice

to serve

sprigs of mint

lemon zest (optional)

Cut the tomatoes into quarters and pass through a juice extractor. Add lemon juice to keep the colour bright, then salt and pepper to taste. Add sugar and Tabasco sauce, if using. Serve with lots of crushed ice, a sprig of mint and a sprinkle of lemon zest, if using.
Serves 4

home-made
tomato crush

Juice extractors are wonderful machines. Fresh foaming carrot juice is my favourite – but try this spicy combination too. You could substitute 2 deseeded chillies instead of the Tabasco sauce, for a fresh, bright chilli taste.

tomato celery and carrot crush

1 kg carrots, chilled

3 stalks celery, chilled

500 g tomatoes, chilled

Tabasco sauce, to taste

salt and freshly ground black pepper

crushed ice, to serve

Push the carrots, celery and tomatoes through a juicer. Alternatively, whizz in a food processor with 250 ml iced water and press through a strainer. Add salt, pepper and Tabasco, to taste. Serve, over crushed ice.

Serves 4-6

campari ruby
grapefruit
whizz

A wonderful drink for a summer brunch party. Serve it as a welcoming drink – one tall glass per person – with a romantic or celebration brunch of toasted brióche with smoked salmon and scrambled eggs garnished with snipped chives. Use ruby grapefruit if you can find them – 2–3 juicy ones will produce this amount of juice. Serve in a huge glass jug so guests can help themselves.

Campari isn't very intoxicating, so this is a perfect drink for early in the day – and great as a pre-dinner drink in summer too.

500 ml ruby grapefruit juice, chilled

4 tablespoons Campari, or to taste

crushed ice

sprigs of mint, to serve

Whizz 250 ml of crushed ice with the Campari and grapefruit juice. Half-fill a jug with more crushed ice, pour in the mixture, cram the top of the jug with mint sprigs and serve.

Serves 2-4

alcohol and coffee

Grenadine is a beautiful jewel red, and made from pomegranates, but you could also use Cointreau, or fresh pomegranate juice, with its slightly bitter taste. (Easy to make – just cut the fruit in half and squeeze over a lemon-squeezer). This is a serious cocktail – if you'd like less alcohol, reduce the quantity of rum and increase the amount of ice – or dilute it with ginger ale.

125 ml crushed pineapple

or pineapple juice

125 ml orange juice

250 ml white rum, or to taste

crushed ice

50 ml Grenadine, Cointreau, or

fresh pomegranate juice, to serve

If using fresh pineapple, peel it first, making sure all the 'eyes' are removed, then quarter and core. Pass through a juicer, or whizz in a food processor (for a chunkier consistency). Place the pineapple juice, orange juice, rum and ice in a blender and whizz. Serve in chilled glasses, drizzled with Grenadine, Cointreau or pomegranate juice.

Serves 2–4

jamaican rum
punch

The spicy tastes in the traditional Bloody Mary are usually provided by Tabasco sauce. The Food Editor of *Marie Claire* magazine makes her own chilli vodka. You could use this instead of the Tabasco for a drink with a bright, clear taste. Test the vodka after 1 day and remove the chilli if it's spicy enough. If not, leave for another couple of hours. Take care, and keep tasting, because you can easily make the vodka too hot!

250 ml tomato juice

1 teaspoon Worcestershire sauce

1 tablespoon lemon juice

250 ml crushed ice

1 lemon wedge

1 celery stalk

chilli vodka

1 bottle vodka

2 serrano chillies,

halved and deseeded

bloody mary with
chilli vodka

To make the chilli vokda, place the chillies in the bottle of vodka and leave overnight. Taste, leave longer if liked, then discard the chillies. Keep the vodka in the refrigerator.

To make the Bloody Mary, place the tomato juice in a blender with the Worcestershire sauce, lemon juice, 1 measure of chilli vodka and the crushed ice. Whizz, then pour into tall glasses and serve with a wedge of lemon and a stalk of celery.

Serves 1

Variation:

Not-very-bloody Mary

A Bloody Mary without the vodka – omit the vodka and chillies, and add Tabasco sauce, to taste. Proceed as in the main recipe.

fruit-flavoured gin makes a **sophisticated** cocktail

blueberry
gin

Sloe gin is one of the great British Christmas time traditional drinks. Sloes – the fruit of the blackthorn – are gathered in the hedgerows after the first frost in autumn and placed in bottles with gin and sugar and set aside until Christmas. I think it should be drunk in small glasses – it tastes wonderful, but is very heady, and can be something of a trap.

Blueberry gin is a variation on a theme. Serve it straight in small glasses – or in long ones with ice and tonic water. Delicious and the most marvellous colour!

Place the blueberries in a large glass bottle. Add the sugar and gin, then shake well and set aside for at least 2 weeks, or up to 2 months. Shake the bottle from time to time – you will see the marvellous rich colour developing as the days go by.

When ready to serve, place a shot of the gin in a blender with 3 tablespoons of crushed ice. Whizz and pour into long chilled glasses. Add a sprig of mint and tonic to taste.

Alternatively, serve alone in small aquavit-style glasses. Do not drive!

1 punnet blueberries

6 tablespoons sugar

1 large bottle gin

to serve (optional)

crushed ice

Indian tonic water

sprigs of mint, to serve

coffee frappé

A wonderful pick-me-up on a hot summer afternoon – and one that can be adapted to other ingredients, such as tomato juice, orange and raspberry juice, pear or apricot nectar, crushed pineapple with some extra juice added, and so on.

6 tablespoons freshly ground coffee

1 litre boiling water

sugar, to taste

4 tablespoons whipped cream

50 g shaved bitter dark chocolate

Place the coffee in a cafetière and pour over boiling water. Let stand for 3 minutes, then pour into a jug with sugar to taste. It should be sweeter than you would usually like. Cool, then freeze in a shallow plastic tray.

When solid but not rock-hard, whizz in a blender or food processor, then pour into cups or glasses. Top with whipped cream and shaved chocolate.

Serves 6

white rum and fresh mango
– a great **tropical** cocktail

Use white rum in this recipe for a pretty, clear summer look. However, I grew up in the tropics and I much prefer dark rum, and would always use it instead. New Zealand food writer Clare Ferguson has come up with a marvellous rum idea – keep 2 vanilla beans in a bottle of rum and use in drinks and for cooking. It smells like the best rum and raisin ice cream!

1 large ripe mango
juice of 1 lemon
100 ml white rum
(or dark if preferred)
sugar for glass
crushed ice

Peel the mango and slice the flesh into a blender. Add the lemon juice, rum and 1 cup crushed ice, then whizz.
Rub the cut lemon around the rim of a glass and press into sugar. Place more crushed ice in the glass and pour over the crush.
Serves 1

mango and rum crush

thick **tropical** crush

This tropical crush is so thick and wonderful it's almost a soup. It serves one as a smoothie, and about six people as a champagne cocktail. Don't forget to chill all the fruits first – but wrap up the very aromatic ones in plastic film to prevent them tainting the other foods in your refrigerator.

tropical fruits such as:

250 g cubed fresh papaya

250 g cubed fresh pineapple

chilled champagne (see method)

sugar, to taste (optional)

watermelon pieces, to serve

Whizz the fruits in the blender with 125 ml champagne. Add sugar to taste, if using. Pour into a chilled glass, and serve with the watermelon. Alternatively, divide between 6 glasses, top with champagne, and serve as champagne cocktails.

Serves 1 or 6

Index